Tilting Ground

A Play

Guy Hibbert

A SAMUEL FRENCH ACTING EDITION

SAMUEL FRENCH

FOUNDED 1830

SAMUELFRENCH-LONDON.CO.UK
SAMUELFRENCH.COM

FOR AMATEUR PRODUCTION ENQUIRIES

UNITED KINGDOM AND WORLD EXCLUDING NORTH AMERICA
plays@SamuelFrench-London.co.uk
020 7255 4302/01

Each title is subject to availability from Samuel French,

depending upon country of performance.

TILTING GROUND

First produced by Peter Cooper at the Mowlem Theatre, Swanage on 7th August 1996, with the following cast:

Nancy	Lisa Davies
Jack	Paul Dubois
Charles	Maurice Thorogood

Directed by James Barry
Designed by Annette Sumption
Lighting Design by Marcus Christensen

CHARACTERS

Nancy
Jack, Nancy's son
Charles

The action takes place on the patio of a large beach house overlooking the sea near Puerto Escondido on the Pacific Coast of Mexico

Time: the present

ACT I

Scene 1

The patio of Nancy's large beach house near Puerto Escondido in the Oaxaca district of Southern Mexico, overlooking the Pacific Ocean

A long run of patio doors US goes into, it can be presumed, a luxurious living-room. There is an outside gate, or entrance. The outdoor furniture is also luxurious, including swing chair, drinks table and rocking chair with a small table beside it. Around the furniture are lush, indigenous plants. To us it is an exotic picture

The music of Falla's "Jota" (arranged for cello) comes through the open patio doors

Nancy, mid-fifties, in light slacks and blouse, comes out of the living-room with a huge vase of flowers which she carefully places on the drinks table, then checks that it is nicely displayed

We hear the sound of a car stopping, and driving off. All Nancy's actions now become hurried, as she picks up a dirty glass and quickly checks that everything else is just so. She hurries back inside with the glass

Jack, late twenties, comes in through the side gate. He wears a light, scruffy suit, a homburg and carries a canvas bag. He drops the bag and looks around. Things have changed

The music is switched off

Nancy comes out

Jack swivels round

Jack (*opening his arms*) Hey!
Nancy (*going to embrace him*) Jack — I can't believe it!
Jack What?
Nancy You're here!

They embrace

At last, you're here!
Jack Yeah.

They separate

Nancy Let me look at you.

Jack takes his homburg off and allows Nancy to look at him

Jack Still got one nose.
Nancy But you've got thinner.
Jack It's the suit. You know, I never could wear suits.
Nancy No, it's not the suit. It's in the face.
Jack Well, I don't feel thinner.
Nancy Maybe it's your hair.
Jack Like it?
Nancy Not falling out is it?
Jack There's nothing wrong with me, Mam.
Nancy I don't care what you look like.
Jack You don't like it.
Nancy Of course I like it. I was so excited when I got your call, I don't know what I've been doing the last two days.
Jack Running around, I bet.
Nancy I wanted to get your room ready.
Jack Know what I've been doing?
Nancy Travelling, I'd imagine ——
Jack Thinking ...

Nancy has heard this before — it's the Jack she dreads

Nancy Oh ... (*Not good*) Good ...
Jack A lot of important thinking.
Nancy Well, that's good ...
Jack (*wiping the sweat off his forehead*) God, the heat in that bus.
Nancy You must be exhausted.
Jack I ran out of beer with six hours still to ride.
Nancy I've just squeezed some fresh juice — that's what you need out here.
Jack Yeah but I've been dreaming cold beer.
Nancy Is that what you want?
Jack I've been dreaming it.
Nancy I've got some Bud, would you like a Bud?

Jack That's exactly what I've been dreaming.

Nancy turns to go into the house

  Did you get it in special for me?
Nancy (*from just inside the house*) The Bud, yeah ...
Jack (*serious*) Mam ...

Nancy stops and turns — expecting an explanation

  I'm sorry. I really am. I'm very sorry.
Nancy (*kindly*) Let me get that beer.

  Nancy goes inside

Jack looks around the patio. He goes to the rocking chair, sits in it and rocks. He then picks up a book from the small table beside the chair. He looks at the cover, flicks through it and then puts it back. He looks out across the beach, rocking

  Nancy comes back with a bottle of Bud and a glass

Jack Isn't that the most beautiful thing!
Nancy The ocean?
Jack Yeah.
Nancy I love it. I love it more and more every time I look at it.
Jack The Pacific Ocean has to be the best.

Jack just takes the bottle leaving Nancy holding the glass

  You've got Pop's chair out.
Nancy Yeah! (*Pause*) You used to sit in that chair for hours when you were small, in the kitchen, remember, a warm stove on a cold night, rocking back and forward, your head in your comics, hour after hour, it used to kind of mesmerize me.

Pause, as Jack tips the beer down his throat, Nancy watches him

  There was happiness written all over your face then. Real happiness. (*Pause*) I never missed him so much all those days and nights when you were sitting there ...

Jack And now we have a hot Mexican sun for a cold Pittsburgh night. He would have loved it here.

Nancy Maybe ...

Jack He would have sat out here drawing up plans to turn this town into something spectacular.

Jack drains the last drop of beer on to his tongue and gets up

I bet you he was going to build up the oceanside and take on Acapulco single-handed. That's what I was thinking when I was coming here, staring out across the mountains — what would Pop have made of this? That's what I was thinking. What would he have done?

Nancy Do you want another Bud?

Jack I'll get it.

Nancy No, I'll do it.

Nancy goes inside

Jack (*noticing something is missing*) Where's the nude?

Nancy The what?

Jack The nude. The statue.

Nancy comes back in with another bottle of Bud

Nancy Oh that — I gave it to some friends. They live a couple of miles down the road.

Jack Pop really liked that statue.

Nancy I know — but I didn't. (*She gives him the bottle*) Why did you do it?

Jack What?

Nancy Disappear.

Jack I've been looking for a man.

Nancy What kind of answer's that?

Jack He was my best buddy and partner and he stole everything I had. I must've been six times round the world.

Nancy Doing what?

Jack Looking for him.

Nancy I don't understand.

Jack He just disappeared. Took off with all my money.

Nancy How much?

Jack My best buddy and partner. We bought some land, to develop some kind of marina, at least I *thought* we bought some land, and then he just took off with my money.

Nancy How much money?

Jack Everything. He took everything. (*Indicating his bag*) This is all I have now. Pop's first suit and his favourite shoes.
Nancy That old suit? You've got that old suit in there? Let me have a look.

Jack unzips the holdall and takes out a crumpled 1940s suit. He gives it to Nancy. She holds up the jacket

My God, you carry this around ——
Jack Yeah, but you've gotta have the shoes!

Jack shows Nancy the two-tone shoes

Nancy Do you ever wear these things?
Jack Sometimes when I'm travelling.
Nancy And this is *everything you've got!*
Jack (*taking a toothbrush out of his top pocket*) And a toothbrush. One thing you can't live without is a toothbrush. You can spend twenty million on a Leonardo but it's worth nothing to you if you can't clean your teeth in the morning.
Nancy Aren't you living anywhere?
Jack I told you, I've been looking for this man.
Nancy You don't even have a room some place?
Jack I've been travelling so much ...
Nancy But all your belongings, your furniture and ...
Jack I sold it.
Nancy Everything?
Jack I had to.
Nancy Everything your father gave you?

Jack is now ashamed

Jack That hurts me more than anything.
Nancy Those were heirlooms. He wanted you to pass them on for when *you* have a family.
Jack I know.
Nancy I mean, you can't put a price on that.
Jack Please, Mam, I *know*.
Nancy Keeping this suit and selling the good stuff, that makes no sense at all.
Jack It was the only way I could pay off my debts.
Nancy You could have called me. (*Pause*) Why didn't you call me?
Jack I'm sorry.
Nancy You know I would have helped you out.

Jack I felt too humiliated.
Nancy And didn't you think how worried I've been? A year's a long time not to call. All you had to do was take five minutes and pick up a phone.

Jack looks tortured

I even had you put on the Missing Persons list.
Jack Mam, I'm sorry. I'm so sorry. I couldn't call you, not until I had got the money back.
Nancy But if you needed help ...
Jack I've let you down too many times before, I couldn't tell you it's happened again. Do you understand that? I can't let you be disappointed in me. Can you tell me you understand that?
Nancy Yeah, I understand that.

Jack takes a dirty handkerchief out of his pocket and holds it out on the palm of his hand

What is this?
Jack Will you forgive me?
Nancy You don't need me to forgive you, Jack. What are you doing?
Jack Take it.
Nancy What is it?
Jack Open it.

Nancy opens up the handkerchief and picks up a gold necklace

Jack takes the handkerchief from her so that Nancy can hold up the necklace

It's for you.
Nancy It's beautiful!
Jack You like it?
Nancy (*admiring the design*) I love it — it's so pretty — are these emeralds?
Jack Yeah.
Nancy I don't think I've had anything given to me as beautiful as this.
Jack Let me put it on for you.
Nancy It's too good for this old blouse ——
Jack I want to see it on.

Jack puts the necklace around Nancy's neck and, now standing behind her, clips it on

Nancy Where did you buy it?

Jack Mexico City.

Nancy I thought you hadn't got any money ——

Jack This took my last dime. (*He looks at her from the front*) Fantastic! You look fantastic!

Nancy I shan't ever want to take it off.

Jack I shan't ever *want* you to take it off.

Nancy (*kissing him*) Thank you.

Charles, early sixties, comes in through the gate. He is dressed in a light suit with a cane in his hand and a panama on his head. He looks like an Englishman in exile should, at least to the romantic — distinctive and eccentric (though something about him always makes him look a little untidy)

Charles Ah, here he is!

Nancy He's just arrived ——

Charles Splendid! Welcome to Escondido.

Charles puts out his hand — which Jack can't avoid shaking

Jack (*mystified*) How are you doing?

Charles Welcome, welcome! Your mother has told me so much about you. Did you have a good journey?

Jack Yeah ...

Charles You took the bus across the mountains ——

Jack Yeah, from Oaxaca.

Charles A wonderful journey, isn't it? A boneshaker of course but quite wonderful.

Nancy goes inside

Charles settles into the rocking chair, with a sigh of relief

Jack looks at him, unsettled by his familiarity

Oh, dear God, that's better! I take a constitutional along the beach every morning. It's very good for pumping the blood. So you flew to Oaxaca?

Jack Yeah.

Charles Where did you stay?

Jack The Santa Catalina.

Charles Was it cold?

Jack Cold?

Charles At night. They say it's cold.

Jack It's de luxe.
Charles But a cold de luxe. This is only what I've heard. And she was a diabetic. Whether that has something to do with it, I don't know.
Jack I wasn't cold.
Charles Oh, well done! Well, I've been looking forward to this.
Jack To what?
Charles Your arrival, of course.
Jack But I don't know who you are.

Nancy comes back with a bottle of champagne and three glasses, and a glass of whisky for Charles on a tray

Nancy (*to Jack*) Will you open this for me?
Jack Sure.
Charles (*receiving his whisky*) Ah, thank you. My medicinal.

Charles gives Jack a knowing smile as Jack starts to open the bottle

Nancy Did you have a good walk?
Charles Juana has had her baby and it is a boy.
Nancy Oh, that's wonderful.
Charles Three-o-seven a.m. There is going to be a party in the Palma tonight. I've put a thousand over the bar for Eduardo and told him we will be in for the hooch later.
Nancy Five girls and now they have a boy.
Jack Oh yeah?
Nancy They must be so excited.
Charles (*to Jack*) You'll come to the party with us of course.
Jack I don't know them.
Charles Good God, you don't need to know people to drink with them!
Nancy They are two of the nicest people.
Charles He is a cabinet maker of the top drawer.
Nancy Juana's a seamstress. She did all our coverings.
Charles We must get them a present.
Nancy They'd love you to come.
Charles Of course they would!
Jack (*opens the bottle*) Are we wetting a baby, is that what we're doing?
Nancy No, this is for you.
Charles One should always have something to celebrate.

Jack starts to pour the champagne into the three glasses

Nancy Of course it's for you.

Charles A gramophone.

Nancy What?

Charles Why not a gramophone?

Nancy What good's a gramophone?

Charles He dreams of a gramophone.

Nancy Who does?

Charles Eduardo.

Nancy It's not his birthday.

Charles (*to Jack*) She gave him all her old Django Reinhardt records —

Nancy He's a big fan of Django Reinhardt ——

Charles But he has no gramophone!

Nancy I want to give them a washing machine.

Charles Give them something they dream about! Who dreams of a washing machine?

Nancy Six children and she doesn't dream of a washing machine?

There's no answer to that ...

Charles Yes, well, I suppose you're right. She's always right, I'm too absurdly romantic to take sensible decisions in these matters. I'll get one sent this afternoon.

Jack The whole town'll be having babies if they hear about this.

Charles We will save the gramophone for his vasectomy.

Jack Are you holidaying here?

Charles "Holidaying"? Can one "holiday"?

Jack Isn't that what you're doing?

Charles I have a permit to reside. I am a *Rentista Inmigrante.*

Jack Where?

Charles Here, of course.

Jack In Escondido?

Charles Of course. My home town!

Jack Who are you?

Charles Jack wants to know who I am.

Nancy (*becoming flustered as she takes the tray of glasses round*) I want to get these glasses round before I say anything — I don't want it to be the wrong moment — I mean ...

Charles You take your time.

Nancy Yes ——

Jack Are we celebrating something else now?

Charles (*takes a glass*) Splendid. Thank you.

Jack (*taking a glass*) I hope you're not going to upset me.

Nancy (*agitated*) Let me just put this tray down — maybe this wasn't such a good idea ...

Charles No-one has to go anywhere. We've all got plenty of time.

Nancy takes the third glass and puts the tray down. They stand in a triangle.
She now realizes that she has organized a rather awkward tableau

Nancy I didn't mean us to be standing quite like this.
Jack So — to whom do we raise our glasses?
Nancy This is to you ——
Charles Absolutely. To Jack's return!
Nancy Welcome home.

They raise their glasses and drink in the painfully unsettling atmosphere

Jack Thank you.
Nancy I just want to say, whilst we are now settled with a drink in our hands,
  Charles and I married five months ago.

Silence — Jack stares at Nancy

Charles Well — splendid! (*Pause*) Splendid.
Nancy There was no way of telling you at the time. We did wait a while,
  hoping that maybe we'd hear from you, and we waited and waited but in
  the end, I mean I didn't know where you were, or when I'd hear from you
  again — I had to come to some kind of decision, we couldn't sit around at
  the end of a phone that maybe wasn't going to ring for another year.
Jack Yeah.
Nancy Do you understand that?
Jack Yeah ——
Nancy I know it's difficult right now, I mean it'll take a while for us, I mean
  all of us, to get kind of used to the idea. I didn't want to have to tell you after
  the marriage but there was no way I could have told you before now. You
  do understand that, don't you?
Jack Yeah, I understand that. That's OK. It's not a problem, is it?
Nancy No.
Jack It's not a problem with me. This is fine by me. Sure. Sure it is.
Charles Well — splendid. (*To Nancy*) That wasn't so difficult, was it?
Jack What? What wasn't so difficult?
Charles Your mother was worried.
Jack Why was she worried?
Charles She was worried about how you would react to the news.
Jack You weren't worried, were you?
Nancy (*finding this difficult*) No, but ——

Jack See, she wasn't worried. She had no reason to be worried. I don't understand that. (*To Nancy*) Are you happy?

Nancy Yes.

Jack Then I'm happy too. See, there's no problem. If she's happy, I'm happy. Why should there be a problem?

Nancy Why don't we go on in and eat? Charles has laid out the most beautiful buffet. He was down the quayside at five o'clock this morning getting the best snappers.

Charles smiles and gestures a certain modesty

You know I haven't cooked a meal in six months. Three times a day all my life I was cooking, now all I do is sit down and there it is, this wonderfully exotic dinner presented to me on a silver platter.

Jack I'm very impressed.

Nancy His cooking is out of this world.

Jack Is that what you are, a cook?

Charles Not by profession.

Nancy He's an actor.

Jack Yeah? What sort of actor?

Nancy A stage actor.

Jack A song and dance man?

Charles (*amused*) I have been known to put on the shoes.

Jack Tap?

Charles Once upon a time.

Jack Oh, I want to see this!

Nancy (*affectionately*) Oh, Jack, not now!

Jack No, I want to see this. I want to see some tap!

Nancy Jack, we're eating now!

Charles I don't have the shoes ——

Jack I just want to see the steps.

Nancy Jack ...

Charles OK, just a few steps ——

Jack Yeah!

Charles (*getting into position*) I'm a little rusty ——

Jack No problem.

Charles Let me see now ...

Pause — then Charles gives a short and gentle but decent enough exhibition of tap dancing. He ends with a little flourish

Jack (*applauding*) Well, you've got a song and dance man who serves up your dinner on a silver platter! Mam, you have hit gold!

Nancy (*enjoying the moment*) I certainly have! Now you come on in and eat.
Jack Did you ever go to Pittsburgh?
Charles No.
Jack New York?
Charles No ——
Jack LA?
Charles I've never been to America.
Jack But should I know you?
Charles I shouldn't think so.
Nancy Charles only worked in England.
Jack What's your name?
Charles Mellor.
Jack Charles Mellor?
Charles It's not a name for the history books, I am sorry to say.
Jack What else can you do?
Nancy Don't ask him to do anything else now.
Jack Just one more thing. I want to hear a song.
Nancy You're not being fair now ...
Jack Only one song.
Nancy (*light-heartedly; to Charles*) However much he had, he always
  wanted more ——
Jack Any song you like. First verse. Then we eat.
Nancy This is not an audition, Jack ——

Charles sings a line from Weill's "September Song"

Jack Oh, I love this one!

Charles sings another couple of lines

Now that is beautiful! I fell in love with a girl who used to sing that in a bar
in Springfields, Illinois. I was passing through and I stayed two months
because of that song.

Jack sits in the rocking chair

Pop used to like that one too.

Nancy goes towards the house

Nancy Never used to sing it though.

Nancy goes into the house

Jack rocks the chair as Charles turns to follow Nancy

Jack Tell me ——

Charles stops

What's a song and dance man doing in Escondido? There isn't a theatre for two hundred miles.

Charles I've retired.

Jack Retired? I've never heard of an actor retiring before.

Charles Most of us just disappear and no-one knows we've gone.

Jack Henry Fonda never retired.

Charles No, I don't believe he did.

Jack I can understand a man retiring from selling insurance but who would choose to stop dancing?

Jack stops rocking the chair and just for a moment they hold an edgy stare before ——

Charles goes inside

Black-out

Jack exits

Charles enters and sits in the rocking chair

SCENE 2

Lights up on Charles sitting in the rocking chair, his eyes closed, a book open on his lap

Jack comes in, carrying two cases of wine. He holds them in front of Charles

Jack Wanna take a look?

Charles (*stirring from his siesta*) What?

Jack D'you wanna take a look?

Charles What is it?

Jack Wine.

Charles For me?

Jack That's what he said.
Charles (*realizing*) Ah, yes! Yes ——
Jack Shall I put 'em down?
Charles Yes, yes, of course. Yes, I want to see this.

Jack puts the cases down

Jack Do you want me to open up?
Charles This is what I've been waiting for. Yes, open up, please do!

Jack starts to open the first case

Has he gone?
Jack Who?
Charles Luis.
Jack Who's Luis?
Charles Didn't he deliver it? You must know Luis.
Jack No, I don't know Luis.
Charles He buys it from Acapulco, you know.
Jack Why should I know Luis?
Charles But you paid him?
Jack He said it was on account.
Charles Oh, I always pay him.
Jack You are paying him — he said it's on account.
Charles I like to give him something else.
Jack What for?
Charles I don't know — delivery, something of that sort.
Jack Isn't that in the price?
Charles Well, it's just a gesture.
Jack I didn't know you paid him twice over.
Charles It's only a gesture.
Jack That's not a usual thing for people to do, pay for something twice.
Charles He's a very friendly chap.
Jack You like gestures, don't you? That's something I've noticed about you. Well, if you can afford it, why not?

Jack opens the case

There we go.
Charles Now, let's see what we've got ...

Jack takes out a bottle and, like a waiter, shows it to Charles

Ah, excellent! Excellent. The Mouton-Rothschild. (*Looking at the other bottles in the case*) Yes, very good — Splendid!

Jack Do you want to see the other?

Charles Yes, let's have it open. They'll do anything for you, you know, these Escondido-ians. A magnificent Paulliac.

Jack Paulliac?

Charles The Mouton-Rothschild.

Jack Apart from cooking and drinking — is there anything else you do?

Charles (*proudly*) Nothing.

Jack Nothing?

Charles Absolutely nothing.

Jack Don't you want to do anything?

Charles What else would I want to do?

Jack Don't you want to build anything?

Charles Build?

Jack Yeah, build.

Charles What on earth would I want to build?

Jack Anything.

Charles Good God, no.

Jack Are you telling me you've got everything you want?

Charles Everything.

Jack You're in paradise, is that what you're telling me?

Charles Absolutely.

Jack (*referring to paradise*) If I could touch that — but it's always just out of reach ——

Jack unfolds the flap of the second box, takes out a bottle and gives it to Charles

Charles Ah, he got it! The '66 Latour!

Jack Another Paulliac?

Charles This is the finest. We'll have this one tonight. A celebration dinner.

Jack What are we celebrating now?

Charles (*handing back the bottle*) The wine. The arrival of the wine.

Jack puts the bottle back and picks up the cases

Jack I'll take 'em down the cellar.

Charles I'd rather you didn't.

Jack It's no trouble ——

Charles I will take them down myself presently.

Jack I've got 'em now.

Charles (*panicked*) Please, I insist.

Jack It's OK ——
Charles No, leave them!

Jack stops

Jack (*lightly*) Have you got a body down there?
Charles If you wouldn't mind putting them just inside the door.
Jack Why don't you want me to take 'em down the cellar?
Charles (*vulnerable*) Because that is my preference.
Jack Why?
Charles The wine is my department.
Jack What, you like to be in control?
Charles Yes. Yes, I do. I have a certain way of doing things.
Jack You like order.
Charles Yes, I do.
Jack So do I.
Charles Then you will understand.
Jack I'll put them by the door.
Charles Thank you.

Jack takes the cases over to the patio doors

(*Now relaxed again*) I like to catalogue them you see. I have a very particular system.

Jack takes the cases inside

Jack then comes back out with a beer and bottle opener — he opens the beer and drinks throughout the next sequence

Jack Were you in a movie called "Phantom Crawler", or "Mauler", or something like that?
Charles No.
Jack I was trying to think where I might have seen you before. Your face is familiar to me. There was an English guy in that movie who had a long yellow tooth and a wolfhound. That wasn't you?
Charles No. (*Pause*) Neither was I the wolfhound.
Jack So give me some of the movies you were in?
Charles I never performed in the cinema.
Jack Why not? I heard that Marlon Brando can get a million dollars just for clearing his throat on screen. And you know something else? He's seventy. See, they don't retire. Did you ever meet David Niven?
Charles Yes, I did.

Jack Does Mam know that?

Charles No reason why she should.

Jack You mean you haven't told her?

Charles No.

Jack You should have told her. How about Sean Connery?

Charles Yes, I've met him.

Jack Him too? But you know all the stars, huh?

Charles I was in the business for thirty-seven years.

Jack You should ask him over. Yeah, why don't you do that? God, the life he must have! Don't you feel like you've missed out when you think of Sean Connery? Think of all those girls and parties and nights of passion that went to someone else. Doesn't that make you hurt? Is he a nice guy?

Charles Yes. Yes he is — but that was a long time ago.

Jack Don't you know him now?

Charles He wouldn't know me.

Jack Have you got any photographs? You know, buddy, buddy, you and the stars?

Charles I disposed of everything before I came here.

Jack (*a sudden edge to his voice*) Then how do I know who you are?

Charles If I had known that my scrapbooks would have been requested here, I would have brought them with me.

Jack So did you only play the guys who stood around pouring drinks for the stars?

Charles I did perform the part of a butler now and then, yes.

Jack At least you got to wear clean shoes.

Charles What attracted me to those parts was more the freshly-ironed linen napkin upon one's arm.

Jack And that's how you got your interest in wine?

Charles That usually comes when one matures.

Charles gets up and starts to gather up his belongings

Jack The king of the one-liners! Is that who you are? The First French Soldier, the Second German Messenger, the Third Policeman on the Left? Why don't you show me the part you played the best; when you walked on, closed the shutters and — walked off. Is it all in the timing?

Charles (*walking across to the table*) Or is it in the walk across the stage?

Jack (*standing in the doorway*) Maybe you are not even king of the one-liners. How could you dispose of everything before you came here? Isn't your life in your souvenirs, everything you dreamed of? You're nothing without that stuff, just an ordinary guy who lived and died and never wrote his name, who never even poured a drink for Sean Connery or closed a curtain for Katharine Hepburn?

Charles I never had the good fortune to even open a curtain for Katharine Hepburn.

Jack I went down to your bar this morning.

Charles I thought you might have been there.

Jack Are you telling me I can't hold my drink?

Charles I am saying nothing of the sort.

Jack I can drink all night and hold my drink.

Charles I'm sure you can.

Jack You are a very popular man there.

Charles I'm glad to hear it.

Jack Signor Mellor has bought something for everybody. And that is one thing both of us have learnt: money makes things happen. And it puts us all into two camps: those who exploit and those who are exploited. The problem is in sorting out who is where. Why did you come here?

Charles Because a plump man had a heart attack in a London lavatory.

Pause

Jack Is that all?

Charles That's all.

Jack That simple, huh?

Charles That simple.

Charles gets up

Jack Where are you going?

Charles To see to my wine.

Jack Are you sure you don't want me to take it down to the cellar for you?

Charles No, thank you.

Jack I'd hate to hear those bottles break — the price you're paying for them. I never heard of wine costing that much before.

Jack stands, blocking Charles's exit

Charles Excuse me.

Jack Henry Fonda was seventy-six when he made *On Golden Pond*.

Charles Yes, a wonderful actor.

Jack What are you, fifty-five?

Charles Sixty-one.

Jack Sixty-one and Henry Fonda was seventy-six.

Jack makes way and watches as ——

   Charles goes inside

Black-out

Jack moves to the swing chair

Nancy enters, sits at the table and places her bag on the floor

SCENE 3

Lights up as Jack leans up against the stanchion of the swing chair, holding a bottle of beer. Nancy writes a letter at the table

Jack Did you know he knew David Niven?
Nancy No.
Jack Well, that's what he said.
Nancy Oh.
Jack You don't sound too impressed.
Nancy What?
Jack I said you don't sound too impressed.
Nancy No.
Jack Wasn't he a pin-up of yours?
Nancy Not a pin-up exactly.
Jack He also said he knew Sean Connery.
Nancy Oh.
Jack Doesn't that impress you either?
Nancy I never liked Sean Connery.
Jack No, I don't suppose you did, not if you dreamed of David Niven. A vegetarian don't dream of meat. (*Pause*) Has he invited anyone like that over?
Nancy Like who?
Jack Sean and David.
Nancy No.
Jack So who has been to visit him?
Nancy No-one.
Jack He must get pretty lonely.
Nancy No, he never gets lonely.
Jack After being around all those famous people all his life, suddenly he's out here, nothing to do, no-one to talk over the good times, not even his photographs to bring out on an evening. I'd be lonely. Does he get any phone calls?
Nancy No.
Jack Letters?

Nancy That's what I'm trying to write.

Jack No letters? (*Pause*) So what happened?

Nancy What do you mean *what happened*?

Jack What happened to him — to cut himself off like this?

Nancy Nothing happened.

Jack How did you meet him?

Nancy I was looking out at the ocean one morning and I saw this figure at the water's edge.

Jack Was he wearing the linen suit?

Nancy Yes, he was.

Jack Leaning on the cane with the panama on the end of his nose? Quite a showman, huh? What was he doing on the beach?

Nancy He was standing with his head up to the sky following the flight of the tanagers.

Jack So what did you do, go down and meet him?

Nancy He saw me looking at him.

Jack So he came to you?

Nancy Yes, he did.

Jack What did he say?

Nancy He said "Will you be my companion, dear lady, for luncheon?"

Jack He said that? Had he met you before?

Nancy No.

Jack But he knew you.

Nancy It was the first time either of us had seen each other.

Jack Yeah, but he must have known something about you. He must have known you were on your own to come straight out with a question like that.

This stops Nancy who now thinks about it ——

Nancy I don't know — perhaps he did. (*An innocent thought*) That never occurred to me.

Jack How long had he been in Escondido?

Nancy Two or three weeks. This is an awful lot of questions you are asking me.

Jack So what was he doing here?

Nancy Passing through. Now will you please let me finish this?

Jack I want to know who I am dealing with. I mean, you've landed a man on me and I want to know who he is, where he's from, what he's doing, why he came here. These are important matters to me 'cos this man is no longer passing through. So you said yes?

Nancy To what?

Jack Luncheon.

Nancy Yes.

Jack And he took you for luncheon and you brought him back here?
Nancy Yes, I did.
Jack And he's been here ever since?
Nancy Since we married.
Jack Sounds just like a fairy tale.
Nancy (*matter-of-fact*) Yeah, that's just how it was.
Jack Did he know how much money you have?
Nancy Not before we married, no.
Jack Looking at this place, he must have known you had something pretty big stashed in the bank. What sort of money has *he* got?
Nancy Now that is not the kind of question one asks. Money is a personal and private matter.
Jack I don't mind telling him how much I've got.
Nancy You haven't got any.
Jack Right, and I don't mind telling him that. I got ripped off a hundred and seventy-five thousand dollars by a man who I thought was my best buddy — and I don't mind telling him that either. He must have quite a bit to pay for all those washing machines he's got scattered around this town. And I can't believe the price of those wines he's got laid down in the cellar. I could get eighty beers for just one of his bottles. That's not bad living for an actor who never made a movie.
Nancy Jack, will you please stop talking about money and let me finish this letter!
Jack OK. (*Pause*) One more question.
Nancy One more.
Jack Can you give me another two hundred?
Nancy You can't have spent that already.
Jack It just seems to have gone.
Nancy You've got nothing to spend it on.
Jack I must've lost it in the night.
Nancy You haven't changed, have you? One step on the sidewalk, you're going one way and your money's going the other.
Jack Are you saying it's my fault I lost out to that guy?
Nancy I have no idea whose ——
Jack The way he took that shirt off my back, I never knew it until it had gone! He was a genius. You can't count something like that against me.
Nancy The fact is you had ——
Jack I must've been six times round the world ——
Nancy I don't care how many times you've been round the world!
Jack You don't believe me?
Nancy I don't know what to believe. You've told me things in the past——
Jack This is the truth. I'm telling you the truth here!

Nancy OK, it's the truth.

Jack But you don't believe it.

Nancy I believe it! But that doesn't alter the fact that you have got through three hundred and fifty thousand dollars in three years with nothing to show for it except a canvas bag and purple socks. You had the chance to put down a business but here you are, look at you, three years on — nothing! Well, thank God your father's not here to see you now.

Jack (*genuinely ashamed*) You don't need to tell me that.

Nancy I wish I didn't. Yeah, you should be ashamed. You don't know what work is, all the time you just play around with the idea of it. And I want to know when you are going to stop behaving like this? It's time you got your act together isn't it? I tell you now, I'm not giving you a hundred dollars every day if all you can show for it is a garbage can of beer bottles.

Jack I'm going to put my head down from now on.

Nancy I've heard that before.

Jack This time it's different.

Nancy It's always different!

Jack Why do you keep putting me down!

Nancy Because you ask me to believe it's different every time you come home.

Jack I'm seeing the world in a whole new way now. Changes are going on.

Nancy Yeah but when do I see them?

Jack Now. It's all happening now. I've got plans.

Nancy You always have plans!

Jack I'm going to do it this time. Believe me.

Nancy Show me and I will.

Jack Right. That's a deal.

Nancy First thing you have to do is unglue that beer bottle from your hand.

Jack Oh, that's nothing. That's not a problem. (*He puts the bottle down*) See, I'm serious about myself now.

Nancy Jack, I'm not trying to put you down, but you've always had fancy schemes and big ideas about everything, they come in with the tide and go out with the tide, you have to do more than talk. (*Pause*) I'll give you a hundred but tomorrow morning we shall sit down and you shall tell me what you are going to do and when you are going to do it.

Jack That's a great idea.

Nancy now puts down her pen, picks up her bag and opens her purse ——

Nancy I'm writing a letter of condolence.

Jack Oh.

Nancy Do you remember Judy Atkins?

Jack From Penn Avenue?

Nancy She died last month.
Jack Judy?
Nancy Brain tumour.
Jack We were born the same day.
Nancy Yeah. Meg and Sam are heartbroken of course. She was *their* only child. When they wrote to tell me, they asked about you, hoping you are well.
Jack Such a pretty girl too.

Nancy gives Jack two fifty dollar bills

Thanks.
Nancy Yes, she was. It should be a reminder to us all never to abuse the good fortune that is our blessing. (*Pause*) Do you understand what I'm saying?
Jack Sure I do.
Nancy Your freewheeling days are over, Jack.
Jack That's right.
Nancy Everyone has to face up to it sometime and you're coming to it late in the day as it is.
Jack Yeah. (*He sticks the money in his back pocket*) Can I ask you one more thing?
Nancy What?
Jack I need a car.

Black-out

Nancy exits

Jack sits in the swing chair

Charles enters and sits in the rocking chair

SCENE 4

Evening

Lights up on Charles and Jack who slouches in the swing chair, drinking a beer

Charles It is true to the word that without one plump man's heart attack in a London lavatory, this conquistador's arrival in a Mexican paradiso would have been inconceivable. I entered his flat at ten minutes past ten hoping to cadge a thumping English breakfast. It was a Sunday and bacon and Bordeaux was our way of celebrating communion. We lived either side of the river. Having each other's keys was a most convenient arrangement if one found oneself drunk in the street in the graveyard hours on the wrong side of town.

Pause

I found him lying on the bathroom floor beside the lavatory. His head was leaning against the receptacle for the lavatory brush, a lump of dead flesh on a pee-stained carpet. William Butler Yeats was beside him, open on pages thirty-four and thirty-five. "Had I the heaven's embroidered cloths, Enwrought with golden and silver light." I can see those lines now and the numbers of the pages, and his face, in one brief moment emptied of a lifetime of discovery. It was a very profound moment. There was a ticket sticking out of his wallet which was sticking out of his pocket, like a mouse. So I took it. Escondido. One way. I'd never heard of the place. It was the one way that appealed to me. The funeral was a very grim affair. Drizzling of course. Roberts and Co., funeral directors, were chewing Wrigley's, pretending not to, throughout the portage of dear John. The gravedigger had a broken zip on his trousers.

Pause

He was an interior designer, my brother, specializing in hotels, and, by one of those quirks of the business world, his talents were hallowed in these ocean resorts. So that is why I came to Escondido, no more and no less than because I came upon a ticket in a dead man's pocket. My only regret is that it didn't happen to me forty years ago. On the day I arrived, the world I left behind ceased to have any relevance. Escondido has freed me from the Basque Separatists in Spain, pygmies, Catholics and Hutus in Burundi, beef wars and butter mountains. I have spent a lifetime collecting the peripheral and ephemeral clippings and droppings of news reporters because the British Broadcasting Corporation and the London Times have duped me into believing that what boozehound, shorthand piss artists say to justify their bar-room accounts is of importance to me. The only information of interest to me is what is happening here, in this deteriorating body of mine, what goes in it and what comes out of it, and here in this house, the degree of comfort in my bedding, the efficiency of my parasol, and out there on the beach, when the tanager arrives on his winter migration and, most important of all, the condition of the snappers in the marketplace. In short, I have become a miniaturist. Why should I want to chase the world? My body will still expire in the lavatory and be manhandled to the mortuary and burnt by people unknown whether I play Lear or Cordelia's attendant.

Pause

Whilst walking along the beach I was distracted by a flight of birds. As I followed their passage inland I saw, in the distance, an elegant lady espying me. She seemed to be not quite real, as if I had placed her there in my imagination. We were drawn together by the hope of long-languishing dreams to be fulfilled. Does that answer your question?

Pause

Jack What was my question?
Charles You asked me why I am here.
Jack You know, we dream the same, you and me.
Charles Perhaps that is taking poetic licence one verse too far.
Jack I don't think so. There is nowhere in the world *I* would rather be than here. You see, we are two of a kind.

Pause. Charles chooses not to pursue this

You know what we should do?
Charles What?
Jack Bond.
Charles *Bond*?
Jack Take in a few bars. Let's do the town tonight, just you and me.
Charles I appreciate the offer but *bonding* is not my forte.
Jack Maybe another night.
Charles Yes. Another night.

Pause

Jack Can I borrow some money off you?
Charles How much?
Jack Three thousand.
Charles (*looking in his pocket*) I'm sure I don't have more than four or five hundred pesos on me ——
Jack Dollars. I mean dollars. I can pay you back as soon as I've got myself organized out here.
Charles I can't lend you that amount of money.
Jack Why not?

Charles Because — it's too much.

Jack Haven't you got it?

Charles Yes but ...

Jack How much money have you got?

Charles A pretty penny.

Jack How much is that?

Charles I inherited a considerable sum from my brother.

Jack So what's the problem?

Charles I can't do it. I'm sorry.

Jack I don't understand. If you've got it, why can't you do it? I don't understand what your problem is.

Charles You should be talking about this to your mother, not to me.

Jack I can't do that because I don't want her to know about this yet. You see, she doesn't think I'm solid on the ground. I understand her thinking that but she doesn't know I've changed. I have to prove that to her now — but I can't get myself organized without a car. I've been doing a lot of thinking and a lot of planning but who takes you for serious when you're selling big ideas going around the place on a bus? Do you understand me?

Charles Yes, I do.

Jack So you'll lend me the money?

Charles No.

Jack You can't turn me down!

Charles I'm sorry.

Jack Sorry is not good enough! She's set you up to this, hasn't she? She's warned you: if he asks for money, turn him away. Well, who are you to join up with her against me? There's ten million dollars here. This afternoon I had to get down on my knees for one hundred. You think I can't handle money, well, you're wrong. I know a lot of things. I've been six times round the world. Most people don't even know they're alive. Nobodies. Nothings. They never will be anything 'cos they've got no vision. Not me. I know how to use this world. (*Pause*) So give me some money.

Charles No.

Charles and Jack confront each other in a tense stare

I'm sorry.

Charles averts his eyes and picks up a book

Jack breaks away

Jack (*throwing his beer bottle away*) Goddamn!

Jack walks out

Silence

Charles looks up, puts the book down. We feel his tension for a moment

Black-out

Charles sits in the rocking chair reading a book

   Nancy enters and sits at the table

SCENE 5

Morning

Lights up

Nancy eats breakfast at the table reading a letter

Jack walks in. He looks as if he has been in the bars most of the night — which he has. He holds a beer in his hand and noisily sits at the table and takes a swig

Jack Why did you give Pop's Django Reinhardt records to that guy in town?

Nancy I never played them.

Jack Yeah but they were his favourite records.

Nancy I wanted to give them to someone who would enjoy them.

Jack He hasn't got a gramophone.

Nancy Jack, you can't tell me I was wrong to do that when you sold off everything he left to you.

Jack I needed the money, you don't. (*To Charles*) Or was it you who gave him the records?

Nancy No, it was me.

Jack On his suggestion?

Nancy It doesn't matter whose suggestion.

Jack (*to Charles*) I think you should buy him a gramophone, don't you?

Charles That's what I've been saying all along!

Jack You need Mam's permission? I thought you had your own money ——

Nancy Will you put that beer down. It turns my stomach to see you drinking at this time in the morning.

Jack puts the beer down

Thank you. (*Pause*) I thought we were going to have a serious constructive discussion today and you don't look as if you're fit enough to tell the time.

Jack You can't talk to me like that just because I have a beer in my hand.

Nancy That was the first thing you were going to change. Can't you remember?

Jack I saw your accounts last night.

Nancy You went through my files?

Jack Beer might turn your stomach but what turns mine is what I saw last night.

Nancy Those are my personal files, Jack. You have no right to go looking around there.

Jack On the twenty-third of every month eight hundred dollars passes from your account into his account.

Nancy That is my business.

Jack I asked him for a loan last night, he said no.

Nancy Good.

Jack My father's money!

Nancy Come on, don't start all that.

Jack He died working for that money. That's what killed him. So who is he (*indicating Charles*) to say no to me! (*To Charles*) He didn't die so you could sit here smelling the flowers and watching the birds and stacking his cellar with fancy wines bought with his money. He'd be mad if he knew about you. He'd be on to you like a lion on a sick gazelle. (*To both*) I've got nothing. Is this how he would have wanted it to be? The one, two, three of us, just as we are now? (*To Charles*) I'll tell you something else, Mr Mellor, he liked his beer. He was like me, my father. We are the same man.

Nancy Why don't you get some sleep?

Jack Why don't you shut up.

Nancy Don't speak to me like that.

Jack Don't tell me to get some sleep. (*To Charles*) You lied to me. You told me you had your own money, talking tall about a brother making you a wealthy man. Aren't you going to bow down your head in shame for lying to me?

Charles Whether your father would have approved of me or not, it is your mother — (who now) ...

Jack Don't even talk about my father!

Nancy Charles, I'll deal with him.

Jack Hey, don't you talk about me like that, like I'm just some travelling salesman you want to get rid of. (*To both*) You think because of this (*holding up his bottle*) I don't know what's going on around me? I tell you, I'm smart. (*To Charles*) And I know who you are. I know why you've never made a movie — 'cos that's something I can check up on. (*To Nancy*) He's not an actor from the English theatre. The nearest he got to Sean Connery was sitting in the front row of the movie house. And he's not retired either. He's working his arse off here. (*To Charles*) Well, you've had a few months easy living out of this but now that's all gonna change. Get up.

Nancy Jack, you can't ...

Jack This is Pop's chair. Get up!

Charles stands up

Nancy It was my decision to give Charles eight hundred dollars. He's never asked me for one cent of my money.

Jack (*picking up the chair*) I don't want you sitting in this chair ever again. (*He starts to take it inside*)

Nancy Put that chair back!

Jack (*dropping the chair*) They don't *ask* you for money for Christ's sake! They get round you like soft warm hands until they get you to *offer* them what they want. (*He now sweeps the books off the side-table*)

Nancy Jack!

Charles kneels down to recover his books; Jack picks up the table

Jack And you can't use this table again either.

Nancy You get out of here now!

Jack Trouble is, you wouldn't even recognize a thief if he had *swag* written all over his bag.

Jack now puts the table down and snatches a book out of Charles's hand

Charles Please be careful.

Nancy You are not staying here a day longer if you carry on like this.

Jack (*reading*) "The Poetical Works of Samuel Taylor Coleridge" (*flicking through the pages*) "Fears in Solitude — The Nightingale" — I bet you never even read a poem in your life till you took on the part of this man Charles Mellor.

Charles Please, be careful — please ...

Jack What? What did you say?

Charles I asked you to be careful.

Jack Of what?

Charles That book.

Jack This?

Charles Please.

Jack Why?

Charles It's very valuable to me.
Jack Just a book.
Charles Please give it to me.
Nancy Jack ...
Jack Will you shut up! I'm doing you a big favour here! Why is it valuable?
Charles It was a gift.
Jack Yeah?
Charles Please ...
Jack Everything seems to be a gift.
Charles It was from my mother.
Jack Nothing about you is the truth!
Charles A Christening present from my mother. It's in a very fragile state of repair.
Jack (*swinging it by its cover*) No, it seems OK.
Nancy Jack, give him the book.
Charles Please ...

As Charles holds out his hand for the book, Jack tears it in half and drops the fragments on to the ground for Charles to pick up

Jack You will not take Pop's place and you will not take his money. What Pop didn't like he bulldozed, and men like you, he just crushed you into the earth. You've been found out and it's time for you to go.

Jack walks out

Silence

Nancy watches Charles pick the pages off the ground

Charles This is going to go on, isn't it?

Silence. They look at each other: the silence confirming what they both fear

Nancy His father was a very cold man. As cold as a father can possibly be to his son. He never got taken to a ball game, he was never asked how school was going. He was never hugged or applauded, they never shared a joke. The only thing he ever gave Jack was money. It became the substitute for everything — and Jack got the best money could buy, the best clothes, the best schools, the best presents — and never so much as an hour of his father's time, even on his birthdays. I loved him as much as any mother could — and more — but there is no compensation for a father who has nothing to give. The excuses soon run out and there is no hiding that kind

of coldness. (*Pause*) And maybe I loved him too much. However strong
my desire to cast him aside, I can't do it. I can't turn him away from here.

Charles Maybe it is time for me to go.

Nancy No. I am not giving in to this. This is my house and my life and I shall
decide who I live with. I want my happiness too. I have it and I intend to
keep it. I will not allow him to drive you away from me and destroy it. We
are going to work this out and see this through together.

Charles goes to Nancy

I want you here and I shan't ever ask you to leave me. Ever.

Charles (*with genuine humility*) Thank you.

They embrace each other, affectionately, but without any sexuality

*Jack reappears in the doorway, holding another bottle of beer — and
watches them*

Black-out

Jack, Charles and Nancy exit

ACT II

Scene 1

Night

Lights up. Another chair has replaced the rocking chair. Silence — suddenly broken by the huge sound of a vibrant tango orchestra belting out a number from inside the house

Jack now comes out, holding a half-empty beer bottle. We can barely hear his voice

Jack Oh yes! My beautiful — beautiful — tango baby! Rosenda! Rosenda! Rosenda! (*To himself*) How do you do it? *How do you do it?* You come out tops every time!

Suddenly the music stops

Hey, what's going on?

Nancy comes out in a dressing-gown carrying a bedside clock

Nancy Do you know what the time is?
Jack Why are you asking when you've got a clock in your hand?
Nancy It's twenty-past three.
Jack Well, that's beautiful ——
Nancy You've woken us up.
Jack The best time of the night — Guess what?
Nancy Keep the music off and tell me tomorrow. Good-night.
Jack This is good news.
Nancy Then I'll look forward to hearing it.
Jack I'm getting married.
Nancy Uh-uh.
Jack Aren't you going to ask me who she is?
Nancy Rosenda.
Jack How did you know that?
Nancy That's a very pretty name.
Jack That's amazing you guessed that, I've only just met her.

Nancy Please don't play any more tapes or sing any more songs or call out any more names. Good-night.

Nancy turns to go inside

Jack Mam ...
Nancy What?
Jack Everything's gonna be all right now.

Nancy goes inside

Jack flops into the swing chair

Yeah — everything's gonna be all right. You see, Rosenda, people, they don't know how to live. They bury themselves under stones. But you and me — we are one and the same. Two people with the same heartbeat. Oh, my tango baby, I will follow you to the end of the world. (*His head flops back*)

Black-out

SCENE 2

Morning

Jack is still in the swing chair, asleep; Lights up

Charles comes in, carrying a tray with his breakfast on it: fresh fruits and coffee. He looks at Jack, stops, thinks about going back inside but decides to stay, puts the tray down and sits. The clatter of the tray stirs Jack

Jack You slept through a very important night last night. (*Pause*) It was one of those nights you walk into as one man and walk out of as another.
Charles That sounds most disturbing.

Pause

Jack It *was* most disturbing. Are you not acquainted with those nights?
Charles Fortunately, no.
Jack Oh God — pure sensation. Rosindi!
Charles Rosenda.
Jack What?

Charles Her name is Rosenda.

Jack Do you know her?

Charles No.

Jack I've met a lot of girls and I've had some good times but, I tell you now, those were just rehearsal. (*He picks up the half-empty beer bottle and swigs*) I once met a girl in some town I was passing through in Utah. Alison. She was from Tasmania, visiting a cousin or something. We met just one night. One perfect night. In the morning she was gone. So I went to look for her. Have you ever arrived in Hobart, Tasmania to try and find someone called Alison?

Charles No, not in Tasmania.

Jack (*getting up*) All rehearsal. Now we start! Yes we do! (*Pause*) You know, like some people have a feel for playing the violin or painting a sunflower, I think you've got the feel for a kitchen.

Charles How kind of you to say so.

Jack I think we should get you one.

Charles A kitchen?

Nancy appears in the doorway

Jack There's some oceanside real estate two miles down from here and I'm gonna buy that land and open a tango bar. This isn't gonna be some chintzy place for country folk out with their wives, nor is it gonna be some ritzy place with bow-tie heavies on the door and craparse balladeers doing their Frank Sinatra. This will be a place where at maybe four o'clock in the morning something happens to you — you've lost count of the beers on the table, the singer is gone on marijuana and cocaine and behind him the tango orchestra soars and dives and then, suddenly, you come face to face with your soul. This is the kind of place you don't come out of until dawn. You've seen through the night and your soul has come alive and you've experienced your whole damn existence for the first time.

Pause

Charles What happens the second time you go?

Nancy And where are you going to find a tango orchestra to play in this town at four o'clock in the morning?

Jack The best time of the night!

Nancy You wouldn't even get one to visit here at the best time of the day.

Jack Hey, don't put me down! This thing wasn't dreamed up in a night. I've been doing a lot of thinking about this. What happened last night was, I found this missing connection. Tango. I had a bar but I couldn't hear the music.

Nancy And who will be paying for this orchestra?

Jack The folk coming in of course!

Nancy Are you sure there are enough people in Escondido who will want to meet their souls at four o'clock in the morning? Most of 'em are building roads at six.

Jack You're always putting me down!

Nancy I'm not putting you down.

Jack (*referring to Charles*) Does *he* have any ideas?

Nancy In fact, for the last couple of years, I have been thinking of investing in some property myself — maybe even developing some land for a hotel or bar.

Jack (*suddenly enlightened*) You have?

Nancy Sure.

Jack Do you want to see this land?

Nancy It's just come on the market, hasn't it?

Jack Last week.

Nancy I thought so.

Jack I went into the agency to check it out.

Nancy That was smart.

Jack I told you I was serious.

Nancy I think I *should* take a look.

Jack I'll take you this morning. (*Now bounding with energy*) Hey! We can create something here, something sensational! This is just what he would have wanted.

Nancy Who?

Jack Pop. This was his vision. To bring this town alive. Turn it into another Acapulco!

Nancy I never heard him say that.

Jack He said it to me. That's exactly what he said to me "I want to bring this town alive". OK! That's fantastic! Listen, I'm gonna take a shower, get freshened up!

Nancy So what time are we going?

Jack Where?

Nancy To see the land.

Jack I'll call back for you in the afternoon sometime!

Nancy You said you were going this morning.

Jack I have a date this morning.

Nancy Ah, Rosenda ...

Jack How did you know that?

Nancy Who is she?

Jack She is unbelievable.

Nancy That goes without saying but who is she?

Jack A violinist in a tango orchestra.

Nancy Oh, I see! This is what it's all about.

Jack Doesn't that sound great? *A violinist in a tango orchestra.*

Nancy You only met her one night.

Jack Most men only have girls like that in their dreams and when they wake up she's gone, and then they pad down to their offices to sort out insurance claims. Not me!

Jack goes inside

Pause

Nancy I'd give all the money I have for a son who pads down to an office to sort out insurance claims and who keeps his dreams as dreams. (*Pause*) Are you all right?

Charles Yes.

Nancy I heard you get up last night.

Charles Jack woke me.

Nancy No, it was before that.

Charles I couldn't sleep.

Nancy I heard you come down here.

Charles Yes.

Nancy And then I thought I heard the outside door close.

Charles That must've been Jack coming home.

Nancy No, that was later. Where did you go?

Charles I just came and sat out here for a while.

Nancy You didn't go out?

Charles It was the middle of the night. I was in my pyjamas. Where would I go?

Pause

Nancy When we first met out there on the beach, when you asked me if I would accompany you for luncheon, how did you know I was on my own?

Charles looks at her: this is the first time she was ever expressed doubts about him

Charles Why ask me now?

Nancy I'm not questioning you.

Charles I had been watching you.

Nancy And what was in your mind?

Charles Everything about you told me you were on your own. You can see it in people — the way you stood there, the way you walked, the way you

looked at me, even in the way you looked out across the ocean. Most of all,
it was in your eyes ——

Nancy I'm not doubting you —

Charles — you saw me like I was flotsam on the beach, a floating wreck
come ashore ——

Nancy No, I didn't see that ...

Charles Wasn't that why we noticed each other and were drawn together —
because we recognized something lonesome in each other? There was no
other thought in my mind except the possibility that we could give to each
other in our last years what we had been missing all our lives.

Nancy How could we have known that?

Charles But we did, didn't we?

Nancy Yes.

Charles Whatever happens to us now, never doubt that our meeting was a
moment of extraordinary chance and profound beauty. Never let that be
replaced with a thought so sordid: that I came to you as a man combing the
beach for gold, a man without any trace of affection and dignity.

Nancy (*putting a hand on Charles's shoulder*) No, I shan't ever doubt that.

Nancy turns and goes

*We hold on Charles for a moment: he looks concerned for the future — but
there is an ambiguity which leaves us sharing Nancy's uncertainty*

Black-out

Charles exits

SCENE 3

Night

Lights up

*Charles, wearing pyjamas and dressing gown, enters and sits in the chair
that has replaced the rocker. He looks out across the ocean*

Jack comes in through the gate

Jack I have been jinxed.

Charles Jinxed?

Jack Yeah, jinxed. Someone has put a jinx on me. She's gone.

Charles Ah, Rosenda ...
Jack Just — disappeared.
Charles You have been bewitched ——
Jack So where has she gone?
Charles — bothered and bewildered.
Jack I can't believe this has happened. I've been to every bar in town.
Charles Perhaps she's gone home.
Jack The hotel's been paid till the end of the week.
Charles Maybe she's gone up to the mountains for a couple of days.
Jack She would've told me. Something's happened.
Charles I'm sure there will be a perfectly simple and innocuous explanation
tomorrow.
Jack No, no, something's working against me. It's a jinx.
Charles Your mother has been worried.
Jack She's always worried.
Charles You were supposed to take her out this afternoon.
Jack I want to know why things can't happen for me — it happens for
everyone else.
Charles What happens?
Jack I was travelling upstate New York, going to visit a friend in Rochester,
it was getting dark and I stopped beside a lake to rest a while and there was
this solid and snug white timber house, snow thick on the roof, chimney
smoking into the sky, logs stacked high beside the porch — and in the warm
orange glow inside the house, I saw this lady playing the piano. She was
so beautiful, so pretty. She was wearing a white blouse, frills all around it,
on the collar and the cuffs — it was a high collar, her back was as smooth
as silk — I could see the line of her breasts inside — Oh God — I walked
up a little closer and I stood beside a silver fir, and I listened to her playing
a tune like from a child's music box. The night was silent and beautiful and
it was just me outside and her inside and the whole damn world some place
else. I wanted to knock at the door and I imagined her opening it and settling
me down beside the fire as if it was where I belonged. She got up from the
piano and then a man came into the room carrying a box of something and
I was back inside the car. I thought about setting fire to the house and
leaving it to burn in the night. But I drove on to Rochester. I'm always
looking at it from the outside. Why should they have that kind of
happiness?
Charles They don't.
Jack I saw it!
Charles It doesn't exist.
Jack Of course it exists! It has to exist! And I am not going to live for anything
less than that. You've got that happiness here. (*Pause*) *I said you've got that
happiness here!*

Charles No-one has that kind of happiness.

Jack Then what have you got?

Charles Sometimes when I walk along the beach, I am overwhelmed with wonder — this astonishing, extraordinary world. And I know then, I know without any doubt, that my spirit will be a part of this creation ever more. But other times when I do the same walk, this same world, everything I see is darkness. I can see death in the shadow of every child on the sand. And I see this tiny and fragile man walking in a vast emptiness towards the water and into the ocean — and he is gone.

Jack What are you saying?

Charles Twenty-seven of my thirty-seven years as an actor were spent waiting for someone to want me. I had failed in everything I meant to do in my life. And then: my brother's death. We were together from my first day in the world to his last. He was the only person alive who knew me. I came here, to Mexico, hoping to find some dignity in life. It was a desperate journey. But in my wildest dreams I did not expect this wonderful thing to happen to me, here. At last I had the chance to live in that happiness and harmony and belonging that I always saw — as you see now — in other people's lives. But that hasn't happened. Everything still haunts me. Nothing has changed. I had thought that by being in another place, I would become another person. You are under the same illusion. If you had knocked at the door of your timber house, you would have destroyed what you had seen through the window the moment the door was opened. You are, like me, searching for heaven on earth, and it isn't here.

Pause

Jack No — no, no, no, no I'm not. I'm not like you. I'm not like you at all. I don't know what failure is. And I don't see death in any shadows for Christ's sake! You think I don't know how to live? You think I have failed in life? What are you saying to me? I'm nothing like you!

Nancy appears in the doorway, in her dressing-gown

Nancy I was expecting you back twelve hours ago.

Jack I'll take you tomorrow to see the land — if that's what you're worried about.

Nancy I had a call from the Missing Persons Bureau this afternoon. Apparently you are in a jail in Richmond, Virginia.

Jack Are they crazy?

Nancy I don't think so.

Jack You don't think so? They've got to be crazy! How can I be in a jail in Richmond, Virginia?

Nancy That's what I thought — so I contacted the jail myself. They said they released you five weeks ago.

Pause

Jack Yeah. Yeah, that's right.

Nancy They said you served one year for assault.

Jack I got some remission.

Nancy So that's why you didn't call me — you were in jail?

Jack Yeah.

Nancy Why didn't you tell me you were in that kind of trouble?

Jack I didn't want you worried about me.

Nancy What did you do?

Jack I hit a man with a rock.

Nancy *A rock* — Who was he?

Jack I don't know. He was just a guy. He was leaning against the coke dispenser at a gas station and he thought he would make a jerk out of me to while away his time.

Nancy What did he do to you?

Jack He looked at me.

Nancy And?

Jack And I didn't like it.

Nancy You hit him with a rock because he looked at you?

Jack I didn't like the way he did it.

Nancy Is that all?

Jack Yeah.

Nancy Just that?

Jack Yeah.

Nancy You don't want to talk about it?

Jack No, I don't mind.

Nancy So how was he looking at you?

Jack He laughed at the way I was wearing my hat.

Nancy The homburg?

Jack Yeah. Then he started looking me up and down, looking at my shoes ——

Nancy What shoes?

Jack My shoes, my two-tone shoes ——

Nancy Your father's shoes?

Jack Yeah.

Nancy Were you wearing his suit you've been carrying around?

Jack I told you, I wear it for travelling sometimes. And he was looking at me like I was a failure, a nobody, so I picked up a rock and I threw it in his face.

Nancy Just because he looked at you?

Jack *He should not have laughed at me!*

Nancy If you had only called me, I would've got you a top lawyer. You needn't have spent that year in jail.

Jack I doubt that. I broke his jaw, I smashed his nose, I split his eye, it was a small town and he was the son of a cop and I didn't apologize.

Nancy When you need help you should always ask for it.

Jack I don't need help.

Nancy You do need help.

Jack realizes that she's implying psychiatric help ...

Jack (*angry*) What sort of help are you talking about?

Nancy It hurts me to think you spent a year in jail and you didn't tell me.

Jack I'll tell you next time.

Jack turns to go

Nancy I went to see that land this afternoon with my lawyer. I've decided to put in an offer.

Jack You have? Well — how about that — it's pretty good real estate uh?

Nancy Yes, it's beautiful.

Jack Didn't I say it was beautiful?

Nancy We both thought it was an excellent prospect — perfect for a top of the range hotel.

Jack You see, I've got an eye for these things. So we're gonna build on it uh?

Nancy The idea definitely appeals to me, and it'll be good news for the town.

Jack That's what I've been saying — it's exactly what the place needs! I'll take you out there first thing tomorrow and show you around.

Nancy Jack, I've already been around.

Jack Not with me. I want us to go together. We're gonna do this thing together.

Nancy If you insist on making that kind of promise, you can't spend all day and night in the bars as well.

Jack Once I've got something to build I don't need anything else.

Nancy OK. We'll go there tomorrow. Ten o'clock. (*Kissing him*) Goodnight. And please get some sleep.

Jack You too. You get some sleep.

Nancy goes inside

Everything starts tomorrow. Tomorrow is day one. (*He turns to Charles*) See? I build. D'you understand what I mean? There's all kinds of building, it doesn't have to be with stone. A man can build by making profit in the market place, in politics, on the football field — or he can make a name of himself in the movies. It's about winning. But I am like my father. He liked to see something going up in front of his eyes, something you can walk into and around and hit with your fist and say "... this is mine, I built this". He and I are the same. And we are winners. We're not like you. (*Pause*) I know exactly what is happening here now. We're propping you up. Without us you'd fall. You're rotten timber and we don't want you spreading that disease in this house. We've got a ten million dollar success here and your presence is a contamination.

Jack goes inside

Charles sits in silence

Jack comes back and stands in the doorway

In fact, it's you who's put that jinx on me. She wouldn't have disappeared if it wasn't for you. So long as you are here, everything goes wrong.

Jack turns and goes inside

Black-out

Charles exits

SCENE 4

Late morning

Lights up

Charles comes in, puts his cane down, takes off his panama and sits in the chair with a sigh of relief

Nancy comes in from the house with a glass of whisky which she gives to him

Charles Thank you.
Nancy Francisco called round about the trees. He says he can come at the weekend and sort it out for us.
Charles (*without much enthusiasm*) Oh good ...

Nancy And Luis phoned to say he's got some — is it Leroche? — Chablis ——
Charles Laroche, yes.
Nancy He says it's just come in and did you want a case?
Charles No, I think we'll leave it for a while.
Nancy Anyway, I said you'd phone.
Charles Yes, I will.

Nancy goes into the house

Jack walks in through the gate. He looks at Charles, who avoids his stare

Jack goes inside

Nancy comes back out with some documents she intends to go through

Jack now returns with a beer

Jack When you go your constitutional you go down here, along the beach and then you take that path up on the hill and when you get to the road you take a right into town, don't you?
Charles Yes.
Jack But you didn't today. You didn't take the road into town today.
Charles No, no I didn't.
Jack Why not?
Charles I felt a little tired.
Jack Oh. I thought you might have seen me. I thought that's why you shortened your journey.
Charles Why should you think that?
Jack Because I followed you. You know I did. You saw me.
Charles Yes.
Jack What's the matter, did I see something I shouldn't have seen?
Nancy Jack ...
Jack Tell her what I saw.
Nancy You didn't see anything.
Jack Shall I tell you who my mother thought that was standing on the oceanside watching the flight of birds with his cane and panama? David Niven. That's who she *wanted* to see. But look what she got — a melancholic man who picks up boys down on the beach every morning.
Nancy I know what happens on the beach!
Jack What a crazy mistake you made out of loneliness and longing for someone else in the house. (*To Charles*) David Niven!
Nancy Don't go on like this Jack.

Jack He gives the little Indian boys money! I saw him! If you know what goes on down there, why is he still here!

Nancy Because he is a wonderful companion to me!

Jack If you had known who he was before he claimed a chair in this house, you wouldn't have taken him in, would you? Come on, you can say it to me, you don't have to put on an act for me. We are family, we fight for each other. You wouldn't have taken him in, would you?

Nancy Nothing happens on that beach!

Jack I have seen it with my own eyes! You can't deny it! You can't pretend it doesn't happen, not any more — because I have seen it! You wouldn't have taken him in if you had known why he is here, would you?

Nancy Go away!

Jack Are you telling *me* to go away?

Nancy Yes, I am. If you can't live here without causing this kind of scene, then, yes, go away.

Jack Because of him? Because you have a man like him in the house? You tell me to go away because of a man like him! How far do you want me to go? Is Pennsylvania far enough for you? Tell me where you want me to go!

Nancy I don't *want* you to go anywhere.

Jack You are telling me to go — for *his* sake? I am *never* leaving here. This is my home and he is not staying. *I do not allow it.*

Jack goes inside

Nancy Perhaps you should go away for a while

Silence

You could stay in Acapulco. I will give you enough money.

Charles Thank you.

Nancy What else can I do?

Pause

Charles Yes. (*Pause*) And would you wish me to return?

Nancy Of course. Of course I do.

Charles I will pack my bags and leave tomorrow.

Nancy (*going to him and touching him tenderly*) You do understand, don't you? He's just spent a year in jail, I can't possibly send him away. (*Pause*) My only child.

Hold a few moments on Nancy and Charles, an image of tenderness

Black-out

  Nancy exits

Charles sits at the table

SCENE 5

Lights up on Charles eating dinner on the patio. We hear Falla's "Nana" (arranged for cello) coming from inside the house. It is a solitary affair

The music is switched off

Jack comes in from the house, holding a bottle of wine. He is dressed like a 1940s American salesman in the dark suit, two-tone shoes and the homburg we saw in the opening scene

Jack You can always tell a man by what he listens to and a working man never listens to a cello. (*He puts the wine on the table*)

Jack goes back into the house

Jack comes back with the rocking chair

Duke Ellington, that's my kind of music. When you've had a long day on the road you want something with a bit of swing, something to lift the soul.

Jack sits in the rocking chair — and rocks, looking at Charles who now eats very uneasily; the longer the silence, the greater the tension ——

I knew this would be a real little paradise. Last time I was here this was just a hole in the ground, the timber was still lying where it was felled and over there, there was a huge mound of stones and some Indians gathered around a dumper truck trying to make sense of the plans. Just like you, Mr Mellor, I was walking along the oceanside here and I knew this was where I wanted to make my home. Unlike you, Mr Mellor, I had to build it.

Silence

Charles now can't eat any more. He glances at Jack

Anything the matter?

Charles No.

Jack So why are you looking at me?

Charles I was noticing the suit.

Jack I bought it when I got my first job out on the road. I was a salesman, Mr Mellor. My father was a man called Michal Perzynski. He was from Katowice. He came to the States in the thirties and worked the mines in Penn. It was a hard life. I was brought up in tenements that weren't fit for pigs but I was lucky because I had an early talent — I could talk my way through doors. One day a friend of my father said "you ought to get into selling, the bullshit you talk" — we laughed about it, but that's what I did. I bought this suit and I went out on the road with a box of meat skewers. You ever been on the road with a box of meat skewers, Mr Mellor? I don't think you have. Meat skewers don't rattle the imagination like, say — Shakespeare. But I worked my meat skewers to the bone to get out of those tenements, never home till midnight, weekends always the longest days and I bought myself a little wooden shack, almost in the suburbs. It was real smart. And I got friendly with the owner of the neighbourhood hardware store, corner of Main and Maple, Mr Alfred Eshelman. He liked my skewers and I married his daughter, Nancy. I fell in love the moment I saw her. Clark Gable and Vivien Leigh. And I have been in love with her ever since. Did you ever know Vivien Leigh? I took over the family business and I turned one store into forty-three with downtown offices in the smartest avenue in Pittsburgh. Forty-three stores, Mr Mellor, from Wheeling to Johnstown. I was quite a big fish in Pennsylvania. And d'you know how I got that big? I worked ninety hours a week for thirty years. Selling nails. There's no romance in selling nails. You don't take an applause for helping people knock two pieces of wood together. I was about to sell out and take my long vacation right here in this rocking chair and watch the sun rise and fall on the ocean. I reckoned I had just about deserved it. One morning I bent down and picked up the mail and I felt something like a bolt of lightning shoot across my chest — and I was dead. Two more months and I would have been here. They had already fixed the guttering. (*Pause*) Come on, eat. (*Pause*) I said eat.

Charles No, I've finished.

Jack No you haven't. I learnt never to leave anything on my plate. Somebody's hard work put that food there and I was to be thankful. So eat.

Charles I can't.

Pause

Suddenly Jack gets up, goes to Charles and fills his glass

Jack Drink it.

Charles Please ...
Jack It's a Latour — the last bottle. I've saved it for you.
Charles What do you mean "the last bottle"?
Jack I've flushed it all, it's all gone, every bottle — except this. Drink it!

Charles drinks it

All of it.

Charles finishes it

Nothing of you is going to remain in this house — not one book, not one
bottle, nothing — Now eat.
Charles I can't.

Jack pulls his head back by his hair and then pushes him forward

Jack You will eat!

Charles eats another mouthful — and chokes

*Jack forces Charles to drink another glass of wine. Then forces him to eat
again*

Charles No — no more.
Jack In this house we always leave a clean plate.

*Jack forces Charles to finish his dinner, forcing the food down his throat (and
his chin) with the help of the wine*

Charles chokes on the food but finally the plate is empty

Lick it. I said lick it!

*Charles is forced to lick the plate as Jack fills his glass again. When Charles
has finished, Jack takes the plate away*

Jack Now drink.
Charles I can't drink any more.

Jack forces Charles to drink — and fills the glass again

Jack I paid for that wine, now you drink it!

Charles Please ...
Jack Drink!

Charles drinks

Did I work my life for you?

Jack fills the glass and forces Charles to drink again

I don't want your clothes in my bedroom, your toothbrush in my bathroom
and I don't want your wine in my cellar.

Charles splutters as Jack tips the wine down his throat

Get up.

Jack forces him to stand up

Now get out. This is not a free house for men who can't get a grip on the
world.
Charles I know you don't mean to be like this.
Jack Go!
Charles I'm sorry.
Jack Don't tell me you're sorry! Get out.

Charles puts his serviette down and walks out of the gate

*Jack stands still for a few moments then puts his hands up to his head: there
is no sense of victory. He can't help himself*

Black-out

Jack moves to the phone and picks it up

SCENE 6

Morning

Lights up on Jack

Jack (*on the phone*) Yeah, a message for a Mr Jack Perzynski from a lady
by the name of Rosenda. ... She's from Argentina. ... Yes, she was staying

at your hotel. ... I don't know her second name. Nothing at all? Are you sure about that? Thank you. (*He puts down the phone*)

Nancy walks in, in a state of shock

Nancy He's dead.
Jack What?
Nancy They've found him on the beach. He was drowned.
Jack Oh, Mam ...
Nancy He must've walked into the sea last night. I told him to go away for a while. He must've thought I didn't want him to come back.

Jack takes Nancy and leads her to a seat and sits her down

Jack Oh, Mam — this is terrible. I can't believe this has happened.
Nancy I told him to go. That's why he did it. That's why he went down to the ocean.

We can see Jack's guilt — we can feel his need to confess

Did you see him last night?
Jack Yeah. He was eating his dinner out here.
Nancy Did he say anything?

Pause

Jack No. (*Pause*) No. He just left.
Nancy When I came back from the doctor, he wasn't here. I thought maybe he had gone into town — I never thought he would do that.
Jack What can I do for you?
Nancy He was a kind man, whatever you may have thought. I didn't care whether he had money, or what he was or wasn't doing before he came here. That didn't matter to me. He was a kind man, a gentle man and you never saw anything happen on that beach did you?
Jack No.
Nancy You shouldn't have said that about him.
Jack No.
Nancy He liked to spend his time with the boys — and sometimes he gave them money — but he never did anything improper, did he? You never saw him do that, did you?
Jack No.
Nancy You should not have said that. He was just a man who wanted to belong somewhere, that's all it was. He talked to everyone because he

wanted to be someone. He wanted to be liked. The boys were just another audience he wanted to entertain.

Jack They seemed to like him.

Nancy Everybody liked him.

Jack Mam, it wasn't your fault.

Nancy I shouldn't have sent him away. I sent him down to the ocean and I drowned him.

Jack He left here last night because — because — it was his decision. It was his decision to go down to the ocean.

Nancy Some nights he read poems to me out here. No-one ever read poems to me before. I always did dream of a man who would do that kind of thing. On a still evening with the moon on the ocean his words used to carry me right up to the heavens. When you find happiness you don't ask questions, you just grab it and hold on to it and pray it will last. And he did give me happiness. In one year he gave me more happiness than I had in the thirty years before that. And he wanted to give me more. He understood what I wanted and he tried to give it to me. That was the first time in my life someone had tried to do that. The first time.

Jack Mam, listen to me. From now on, I'm gonna be here. I'm gonna settle down and look after you. I'm taking over. That's what Pop wanted me to do. That's what he told me. We're gonna have a good time and we're gonna be a great team. When we buy that land we're gonna build on it together. Everything we do, we do it together. And I'll take you anywhere you want. If you want to go to the mountains, we'll go there. If you want to spend some time in LA or some place, we'll go there. I'm looking after you from now on, OK? D'you want me to start with some coffee? Let me get you some coffee. OK? Mam?

Nancy cries silently

(*Consoling her*) Hey, Mam — c'mon — I'll see you're all right. I will. I promise I will. It's you and me from now on. Just you and me.

Jack stays with her, comforting her

Black-out

Jack and Nancy exit

Scene 7

Morning

Lights up. The phone is ringing

Nancy rushes out of the house to answer it. She's dressed for a funeral

Nancy (*on the phone*) Hallo? ... Jack! Where are you? ... Where in Argentina? ... You're looking for Rosenda? ... No, I'm OK, I'm just about to go off to the funeral, I'm waiting for the car to pick me up now. ... No, I'll be all right, really. ... Have you got a number you can give me where I can contact you? ... Well then, will you give me an address as soon as you have one? ... No, I'll be all right, just make sure you call me. ... I love you too. ... Goodbye ... (*She slowly puts the phone down*)

Nancy looks out over the ocean

The doorbell rings

She stays out for a few moments longer, takes a deep breath and walks out

Slow fade out. All that's left is Charles's walking cane

FURNITURE AND PROPERTY LIST

Further dressing may be added at the director's discretion

ACT I

SCENE 1

On stage: Swing chair
Drinks table. *On it*: dirty glass, selection of drinks and glasses
Rocking chair. *By it*: small table. *On table*: books
Plants
Telephone

Off stage: Large vase of flowers (**Nancy**)
Canvas bag. *In it*: 1940s suit, two-tone shoes (**Jack**)
Two bottles of Budweiser beer (opened), glass (**Nancy**)
Walking cane (**Charles**)
Tray. *On it*: bottle of champagne, three champagne glasses, glass of
whisky (**Nancy**)

Personal: **Jack:** toothbrush, dirty handkerchief. *In it*: gold/emerald necklace

SCENE 2

Re-set: Book on table

Strike: Canvas bag
Tray, bottle of champagne and glasses, whisky glass
Two bottles of Budweiser

Off stage: Two cases of wine (**Jack**)
Bottle of Budweiser (unopened) (**Jack**)
Bottle opener (**Jack**)
Handbag. *In it*: purse with two fifty dollar notes (**Nancy**)

SCENE 3

Re-set: Bottle of Budweiser by swing chair

Set: Letter writing materials, pen on table

Scene 4

Strike: **Nancy**'s handbag
Letter writing materials

Scene 5

Set: Nancy's breakfast, letter on table

Off stage: Two bottles of beer (opened) (**Jack**)

ACT II

Scene 1

Set: Chair in place of rocking chair

Re-set: Books on small table

Strike: Empty bottles
Nancy's breakfast and letter
Rocking chair

Off stage: Bottle of beer (opened) (**Jack**)
Bedside clock (**Nancy**)

Scene 2

Off stage: Tray. *On it*: fresh fruit breakfast, coffee (**Charles**)

Scene 3

Strike: Tray, breakfast, coffee cup

Scene 4

Off stage: Walking cane (**Charles**)
Glass of whisky (**Nancy**)
Documents (**Nancy**)
Bottle of beer (opened) (**Jack**)

Scene 5

Set: **Charles**'s dinner, wine glass, serviette

Off stage: Bottle of wine (opened) (**Jack**)
Rocking chair (**Jack**)

SCENE 6

Strike: **Charles**'s dinner, glass, serviette
Bottle of wine

LIGHTING PLOT

Property fittings required: nil
Exterior. The same throughout

ACT I, SCENE 1

To open: Daylight effect

Cue 1   **Charles** goes inside   (Page 13)
             Black-out

ACT I, SCENE 2

To open: General daylight effect

Cue 2   **Charles** goes inside   (Page 18)
             Black-out

ACT I, SCENE 3

To open: General daylight effect

Cue 3   **Jack:** "I need a car."   (Page 23)
             Black-out

ACT I, SCENE 4. Evening

To open: General evening effect

Cue 4   **Charles** puts the book down. Pause   (Page 27)
             Black-out

ACT I, SCENE 5. Morning

To open: General morning effect

Cue 5   **Jack** watches **Charles** and **Nancy**   (Page 31)
             Black-out

ACT II, SCENE 1. Night

To open: General night effect. Dimmed light from inside house

Cue 6   **Jack**'s head flops back   (Page 33)
                Black-out

ACT II, Scene 2. Morning

To open: General morning effect

Cue 7   **Charles** looks concerned   (Page 37)
                Black-out

ACT II, Scene 3. Night

To open: General night effect

Cue 8   **Jack** goes inside   (Page 42)
                Black-out

ACT II, Scene 4. Late morning

To open: General late morning effect

Cue 9   **Nancy:** "My only child." Pause   (Page 44)
                Black-out

ACT II, Scene 5

To open: General daylight effect

Cue 10   **Jack** puts his hands up to his head   (Page 48)
                Black-out

ACT II, Scene 6. Morning

To open: General daylight effect

Cue 11   **Jack** comforts **Nancy**   (Page 50)
                Black-out

ACT II, Scene 7. Morning

To open: General daylight effect

Cue 12   **Nancy** walks out   (Page 51)
                Slow fade out of general lighting

EFFECTS PLOT

ACT I

Cue 1   To open
         *Music of Falla's "Jota" (arranged for cello) can be heard through the
            patio door*

Cue 2   **Nancy** places vase on table   (Page 1)
         Sound of car stopping, and driving off

Cue 3   **Jack** looks around him   (Page 1)
         Music is switched off

ACT II

Cue 4   To open   (Page 32)
         Music of tango orchestra from inside the house

Cue 5   **Jack:** "... tops every time!"   (Page 32)
         Music stops

Cue 6   Black-out   (Page 45)
         Music of Falla's "Nana" from inside the house

Cue 7   When ready   (Page 45)
         Music is switched off

Cue 8   Black-out   (Page 51)
         Phone rings

Cue 9   **Nancy** picks up the phone   (Page 51)
         Phone stops ringing

Cue 10   **Nancy** looks out over the ocean   (Page 51)
         Doorbell rings

www.ingramcontent.com/pod-product-compliance
Lightning Source LLC
LaVergne TN
LVHW051805080426
835511LV00019B/3415